The Love of Strangers

The Love of Strangers

MICHAEL SCHMIDT

Hutchinson
London   Sydney   Auckland   Johannesburg

First published in Great Britain 1989 by Century Hutchinson & Co Ltd
Brookmount House, 62-65 Chandos Place, London WC2N 4NW

Century Hutchinson Australia (Pty) Ltd
89-91 Albion Street, Surry Hills, NSW 2010

Century Hutchinson Group (NZ) Ltd
PO Box 40-086, 32-34 View Road, Glenfield, Auckland 10

Century Hutchinson Group (SA) Pty Ltd
PO Box 337, Bergvlei 2012, South Africa

Photoset in Linotron Times
by Rowland Phototypesetting Ltd,
Bury St Edmunds, Suffolk
Printed and bound in Great Britain by
Anchor Press Ltd, Tiptree, Essex

British Library Cataloguing in Publication Data

Schmidt, Michael, 1947.
  The love of strangers.
  I. Title
  821'.914
  ISBN 0-09-173887-3

For Donald Davie and C. H. Sisson

So, if one can keep oneself out of it, one may present a picture of a
sort of world and time.

Ford Madox Ford, *Return to Yesterday*, 1931

The Love of Strangers

I

Easy to love the dead! So I love you more each year,
More tenderly, precisely draw you back
Into your landscapes – they ached without you . . .
Your orchard of emerald domes and spires, of fruit
With pebbly skin, grown from the sticks you brought
Out of the clouds around Atlixco, Puebla.
Fuerte they called the tree
That stood against Pacific frosts
And learned to yield crates of fat fruit each season.
In that high village where you found the bud-wood,
Below the snow-line, New Spain's first poet
Endured her childhood: little bastard
In her grandfather's rustic library, somehow
Clutching a quill at his long table, 1660.
If I say I am fair, I say no more than is true;
Your eyes attest I am, my deeds prove me so.
Fair! That great medallion at her breast,
And shrouded (like your one daughter) in nun's habit!
A saint, severe from love and abstinence.
With her you shared thin air, dizzying vista –
Not century, language, faith. Severe you were,
From love as well, without theology, so that you died
In a night ward restrained by nameless sisters
And your ashes were salted over the rusty hectares
Of my godfather's poor ranch in Tamaulipas . . .

I draw your little airplane edging along the Cuban coast
Like a moth enraptured by a sunlit velvet sleeve
Spread on an endless shelf of white-flecked blue.
You landed on an army polo field,
The horses crazed and rearing as you taxied,
The officers indignant, curious . . .
Havana as it was, you the first human bird ever to land
In that promiscuous opulence. You'd flown across
From sober, parched Yucatan. Big headlines
Announced that Cuba was much less an island . . .
Banquets, and the women. 'No papaya for me,' you said,
'I do not take to it.' Bursts of laughter behind fans,

Your host in a loud whisper, '*Fruta bomba!*
Here papaya has another meaning!'
                              Beyond gaping arches,
Steep cliffs of ficus, florifundio,
The shanties had another meaning, singing, Guillén's
Barefoot island ripened in its gullies, its sweet fields:
I'll drink you in a single gulp, dark girl, dark night;
Take off your robe of foam!
                              In my billfold
I have a photograph of you: 1919, Maracaibo Bay.
A pipe's clenched in your teeth.
You lean on the tiller of a little boat.
Who held the camera? *It's time you came back home*,
Your road is going wrong . . . (Martí, the poet).
I recognize the rage stored in that frown,
Which burst, the way that fire destroys a cloud,
Chasing wild echoes round a hemisphere
And rain for days.
                              Then the California landscape,
A mortal splendour, you belong like the mountains,
The sea, far from the thickening centre, snared by no man.
My first memory's there: Capistrano,
The Big Acre, the avocado plantings,
Dragging old orange trees out with a fork truck,
Their short roots thick and squat like the roots of teeth.
Our reservoir, the rattlesnakes alarmed along furrows.
Gophers raised domes among the vegetables,
Pulling our well-grown asparagus
Stalk by stalk into their vaulted cellars. At night
Skunks with steaming broods crawled under the house;
We had to poke them out with sticks and shoot them.
We had a jeep and eucalyptus trees. How hot
All the days were, red grapes got ripe for the ants,
And the low house was haunted mornings, evenings,
By you, tall and dusty from your work.
                              That world ceased
When we moved back to Mexico, you sat down once more
At your big green roll-top desk and the heavy ledgers.
The truth is, you were continually outliving
Your fantasies – or you ran short of money.
Enchantments failed. We were growing old. I was five.

At sixty your liberty had ended.
Sixteen years till your death – and the pain of losing
Year by year both memory and illusion. The boy
With the terrier who was such a superior ratter
In Torreon; in Aguascalientes, the massacre of the Chinese
When Villa was afraid to occupy the town
The Federals had deserted, leaving common folk
To their revenges, and your dad quickly
Boarded up the shop and hid as many Chinamen
As fit in cellars and attic; the Dictator
Three years earlier, omnipotent, relaxed,
Passing where you and your cousin Howard
In short trousers squatted fishing by the canal
At Xochimilco, and the old copper-faced *caudillo*
Smiled in the flowered barge, saluted you back . . .
They got forgotten in the grim refrain
'I have about ten more years'; then the refrain
Got forgotten and you started coasting.

When you were a captain at the end of the First World War
– It's there you learned to talk like Teddy Roosevelt –
You went to France for the first and only time
To help assess the war debt. You saw Verdun
Where every inch of soil was overturned
And suddenly you were glad God hadn't answered
Your boy scout prayer for 'action'.
But when you're old things change;
An old man longs to have died young.
You would have done it well, and left behind
Hearts that only time and money mend.

And something remains apart from what you spoke of,
Something that's mine, I can't be sure of it.
                    Who showed me – it was you –
The great black rose window in some chapel –
And the Sequoiahs, did I go down on my knees?
And here below, a sad, a shadowy house . . . and who is she?
I came – I must have come – full of love and my cot
Was cold, the room was cold. There were bears and creatures.
Time passed, you were the long hand of the clock,
Morning and evening, morning and evening, time went by

13

With its feasts, its toys and solstices, till rose
And cold room were memory and less than that,
An almost deadened nerve; but the gilded cornices,
The steep sash, the sickles of the trees come back
Now that I have a son. How cold is his room?
I am standing tall myself
As a grandfather clock.

       If it were not for time
We could be brothers, the three of us.
As it is I feel your cheekbones in my smile,
Your gestures bend my arms and wag my head.
The pure tone of your whistle finds my lips
As if I was an echo, a reflection,
And you stood over there with your neutral smile
Watching what time, not silvered glass,
Does to the very last of your sloughed skins.

         Half of my life you've been dead
And yet not absent for a single day! I steer continually
By your prohibitions. 'Dear Papacito', school letters began
When most of the time I meant to wound. After all,
You'd sent me four thousand miles into exile
And called it education. I had grievances. I hurt you
Because you were too guileless not to trust me.
You wadded up draft after draft of your replies
But kept my letters in a drawer
In your steel roll-top desk at Pino 458.
After you died I found them stashed there
As if they were love letters. But this is the first.

II

If I'd known how well, after your death, I'd come to know you
That day you climbed four flights (and you almost eighty)
For an interview in Churton Place,
I would have taken more attentive note;
And the time we taped you down in Maiden Newton –
Late winter, pitch dark at five, thorned boughs across the door –
And caught your rusty voice doing 'Gloriana
Dying', with you dying . . .
My heart wasn't in it.
                        Now she's in deep:
You may imagine you're dead. I tell you different.
If dead, what are these spells you still weave? If dead
Why are you so indiscreet, your secrets spill
Like leaves from a frost-stung tree, with besom and basket
She gathers facts, as if such truth really mattered.
It puzzles me how you kept no secret from yourself,
You were your chronicler and stood in your own eyes
Naked as a girl half-loved, distrusted.
                                    Wanting to write of you
I write of her. She climbs with her bright youth into your frame
And both of you are altered – merged? Married, is it?
She borrows your irony, or is borrowed by it;
Your styles were made for each other, but I love only her.
Just now she's away in your house, sleeps in your musty room
In the bed you died on, loved on, and she gives you
– You were a white witch – house room, heart room.
I say the rosary of her absence, doubt's *pater noster*
Meanwhile.
                You called me a rogue, your rogue cat liked me,
Sat on my lap, stitched me gently with his claws,
Needling, needling, hinting what he might do.
Was his name Tib, or Titus? Is he still alive,
Bleached by years, as you were: white witch, white cat . . .
I say the rosary of her absence, she sleeps in your bed
Under coral rug, sea-blue counterpane, and moonlight sends
A foliage patchwork, webbing her face with summer,
Years of summer.
                    Jealous of the dead! No, afraid rather

15

Of her new intimacies. Oh, you had family,
They survive: cousins, eager of tongue, amiable,
Loving, loving.
                    Also a coven of friends
Strayed now through England. She makes her way
Like a nurse among them, nodding, smiling, noting symptoms,
Or like a good daughter in search of you
In the stale upper air where memories embroider the shroud.
Which is she, nurse or daughter? Daughter or wife?
The story of your life displaces hers, rebarbative,
And will not merge.
                    Release her back to me:
What sacrifice do you require?
I cannot share with you: she is not Proserpine,
I am not Dis. She ate the fruit I offered whole, without remorse
Till latterly. I claimed her by contract where I named her –
Hardest of all to love, best loved of all.

III

One by one your friends
Fell to the force of sensible arrangements,
Sowed themselves in prosperous soil and grew
Their various houses. In the high windows
Children's faces showed, and they came down.
We aged, our taproots deep in compromise
And money. We have become a benign forest now,
A little jealous of your doubtful liberty.
We patronize you as we do the memory
Of our own youth, as though you were a child
Who touched in us a silted innocence.

Free spirit! Free within this loving forest
Where you are home a few more easy years –
If there were a room here large enough
It would be yours for ever, as we are.
But can you settle with those words that are
Air and your air, and on what countryscape
Whose shapes conceal the lover that you seek?

IV

'He's in a home now,' Mr Stringer said, and with distaste,
'He shares a room with somebody.' He sank lower in his chair.
I sucked my drink and wondered:
                                    what of his sons,
The impatient, youngish wife? He was impossible
And vain, but you got used to that. Perhaps his last marriage,
Apparently for love, had been a one-way street, he doting,
She comfortably killing time while years and illness
Made a meal of him.
                        Unkind, I chided myself.

                                              But did he merit
A final Home alone, coupled with a skeleton this time
Unchosen, and crippled so he could not crawl
Into a little limelight – go out at one of those soirées
With the comforting celebrity that friends provide
Who used to clap his poems and drink his wine?

'He'd got hard-up, I knew.'
Mr Stringer nodded. 'Got hard up.'
That he'd fallen all the way surprised me:
He'd been so prudent in earlier marriages,
As widower husbanding his shares, erect at his huge desk,
Lost in the contrived disorder of journals, books,
Paced by the local pulse of church bells, pen busy
With thin and thinner lines, then busy still with nothing.

'I last saw him when they changed his hip.'
'That's a good ten years back now.'
He lay in a private bed so frightened of pain, of dying,
That his eyes pleaded like a child's.

'In 1968 he welcomed me.
He dubbed me Facilitator.
I was to redress his quarter century's neglect.
I took him at his word, then had the task of letting go.'
'Oh, I knew him before the War, we sat it out together.
Both C.O. We're contemporaries, if anything,
I'm the elder.'

What was the absence in his novels, poems?
Always *a table for one*, silver and crystal, the glow
Of pale candles, pale eyes focusing desire, but furtive,
Unable to name the heart, to lay a hand on the heart,
But in the mind's ferment, hard breasts, intelligent thighs.
Always a table for one, but large, with places laid
For those the mind invites, whose white unblemished flesh
Becomes momently real – then vanishes, not even a scent
Staining the intellect.

        'He always had a certain clarity.'
The clarity of platitude. 'But, poor chap,
He got his timing wrong.'
He abandoned his native Ulster – 'a black book
I never want to re-open'; but the Troubles made a fashion,
He took the volume down and dusted it. Too late for homing,
He left a page turned down just in case.
He aped Continental radicals, but gave them up
Years before their crossing from Dieppe.
He could always say (and did), 'I'm an Ulster poet'
Or 'I passed that way some time ago.' True,
But he never stayed.

        Chameleon! like Derain –
A quiverful of brushes, travelling each fashionable highway,
Altering his palette in ways that passed for genius
And sometimes was. This age is less generous. I've never known
A man so worldly, the right books on his shelves
If he could only lay his hands on them,
Cursory, eclectic, his optimism
Naive jetsam of a precocious childhood. By running on before,
Then running back with stale 'I told you so's',
A sort of prophet after the event, he passed as wise for a time.

In retrospect he must have drawn a hundred times the map
That leads to his blank bed, his faded page.
On principle he avoided the War but it took everything;
His history stopped at 1938 – annus mirabilis, the novel,
The great success that History swallowed.

        A man so eager
To catch the boat, and the boat pulling away, leaving him
With his trunk and hopes on the quay! He amazed me the first time
With his urbanity. Later he trotted out the same anecdotes

Like a soldier who chews your ear with one old battle.
Each time I went to his tall gilded flat he had
Something urgent to show me he just couldn't find
On those sagging shelves of literature, and evening
Folded us into dim armchairs, whiskies in our hands and him
Still talking, unwilling to let go.
                                    The last time, too,
Reluctant to be seen, grimacing, tear-maps on his cheeks,
Then holding my hand in both of his and asking,
'How good am I? Tell me, how will my work be taken?'

                                    Pain's grown like a tumor . . .
Now he's a single knot of it or empty altogether.
I cannot visit him. He's too worldly to be seen
Shaved of vanities, naked on the quay for the little ferry boat
That this time comes to take him – is it to Ireland?

Mr Stringer rises. 'Time for dinner.'

Where I am as where he is the January air is cold,
Such lights as burn are not reflected by the lapping water.

V

If he'd been a bird he would have had no feathers:
Sharp beak, sharp talons, a voice pure as water
Just at freezing point, or the mind at sleep
On the point of transformation.
                                His last book's inscribed
Plein d'amitié – Janos Pilinsky; the first was fuller:
Plein de remercîments et d'amitié: du sollst mich nicht
Vergessen. That's how we talked in Babel, trading phrases,
The small change of language. Yet he meant it.

I tease out an image of yours: how she wipes the mirror,
For it strikes her that the frame is beautiful;
The glass should be worthy of it, of the room.
She polishes the dust away, the cobwebs,
Stands back and is rewarded by – herself.
Aproned, red-faced, her hairy arms and lip.
'At least the job is done.' 'At least it's true,
The thing she sees.' 'It's not the thing she sought.'
'She was not seeking, really. Was she seeking?'
'Not really, but like Picasso said, she found;
Like Saint Teresa, she found it in the stew,
In menial circumstance, in dailiness. She looked
And was dazed by the visual irony –
The gilt about *her*! The carved fruit and leaves
Framing the least servant, I forget her name.'
As if a murderer found he wore a halo
And was borne by an archangel at each hand.

You were borne by angels till they dropped you:
The army of heaven has become so clumsy.
You are dead now and I don't forget you,
Or how you startled yourself, incongruous
But real in the frame of every poem.
You were after gravity, and earth,
But found the rags of spirit on the wire,
And found the wire, too, and the flanking trench.

VI

He organized the crazy assault on Trotsky
In Coyoacan, he and an artists' gang,
But History had asked the victim out to dinner.
When Trotsky died, no artist held the spike.

He would happily have broken his neck to paint
A Sistine ceiling worthy of dear Stalin.
Not a single image of love! A better artist said
What we wanted we wanted without innocence.

Dead now – revolution's pimp, acrylic
Vandal, pornographer of ideology . . . Buried!
The ill-primed surface of skyscraper murals
Spills his genius in a steady drizzle of flakes.
I am an architect of clouds. Dustclouds.

Before his release from Lecumberi 30
I had myself driven each month to the prison,
Sat lovesick in my father's car and pined.
The chauffeur kept the engine ticking over.
In a sunlit cell at the front, where the big pirul tree
Brushed the tezontle with its plumes and seeds,
He was painting (I thought) in a light we shared.
He soured me against all I was made of,
All I would love.
                                When they released him in '68
I got myself invited to the opening at Misrachi's
Of his prison pictures. These images were new:
I'd never seen his surfaces up close,
His coarse, hacked lines, paint thicker than skin,
Seared, sold before the flaying was complete . . .
Faces boiled, each finger broken – butcher more than painter:
If he'd been given our actual bodies, with his palette-knife
What would he have made of my father and me?
The *organ of our syndicate*, he wrote, was *El Machete*.
He dreamed of leading *organized masses*.
His pictures sold to American collectors.
                                And here he was,

Out of his cage, short, shaggy, scented with Right Guard,
Lean-faced but the body stout with long confinement.
He autographed catalogues with a Pepsi biro.
I waited in a queue, watching for the man
Who had led the revolution of the image,
Commanded Orozco and Rivera, erased the names
Of *individual painters* as too bourgeois.
When my turn came he wrote
David Alfaro Siqueiros
In inch-high characters.

Orozco, while a boy, was maimed in an explosion.
He lost a hand, his eyes were damaged. Out of pride
He had to be an artist anyway, out of love and pain.
Rivera learned to paint because of women, stones and mirrors.
Again it was Leda and Lethe. It was Narcissus.
Both men outgrew Siqueiros. Artists don't want leaders.
Revolution, Orozco said, *paints no pictures*.
He left the syndicate with half a dozen others.
We all fell out with Siqueiros.
                              Why can't I put out of mind
Those coiling gourds of his last prison period,
Those gourds that twist on their rough dish
And rise, as if they grew
From that captivity into the world
His revolution has not made?
And there were zinnias, white fire, walls
Falling, rifles, bones; he grew
Into himself in prison, like Genet,
Holding a brush in one hand and his hard
Penis in the other, not for love:
Art of a damaged son, child of a damaged land,
Pygmalion, making a thing he must control,
Praying History to put colour in its cheeks.
When it steps free of the easel will it speak
From his own lips? Muddying his palette
With rage and desperation, his changing heart
Was never in this world.
                              Architect of clouds.

VII

I knew a tired old man in Islington.
'History skirted me, we never actually met.
Not really. Not in France, and not in Spain.
I was too clever for it: look at me.
I've lived this far.' By that, he seemed to mean
Too long, the way survivors do who clutch
Tight to life, in terror and resentment.

History grazed him, anyway. He lost
All his friends and one eye in the trenches;
Then a wife back home. Spain harvested
A second generation. Madrid he could remember, '37 –
Steep ruins, corpses, and the writers' prattle.

He surrendered to the Party, mind and pen,
As an acolyte embraces a dark priesthood
Out of a hunger for the crucified,
The passion of a man whose single pain
Longs for the facelessness of commonwealth.
He burned his future while his foes burned books.
They burned men, too; but so did his comrades. Winter
Frothed like grave alyssum on the wound.
The hole was never filled in: was a mouth
Bearded with foliage, without a tongue,
Receiving every year new generations,
Green tribes, raw heresies that tasted sweet.
Who ever heard of graves with such a hunger?
It was all a mad idea, except the hunger.

In 1956 he drew the line. Until then
The idea usurped his skull, translating
Justice, love, into its idiom.
Even when he broke faith it held him:
He repeated parrot-fashion stupid things
He must have known untrue, he had no energy
To start again, there was no place to get back to,
Nowhere, even though he was the first
English pilgrim to Rimbaud, he raised Donne from the grave

And brushed him down, and said 'Remember Swift,
He's neither dead nor sleeping – we are.'

When I first met him, at a little dinner party,
He was inaudible, stared at his hands.
He almost could not see them even then,
Fumbled with them, as if memorizing.
Three years later he took shape for me,
Obliging, as a tree will fill with leaves.
I shaded there trustingly, we talked,
Teasing memory, drinking his vodka.
'*I can remember much forgetfulness*,
As Hart Crane said if I remember rightly . . .
I printed some of his poems, and once I met him
In London, did I tell you?' He had told me,
And written 'Poets' Fare'. I said he hadn't.

One weekend in his native Essex
We went to the coast. Blind then,
He pointed back the way we'd come and said:
'Out there you'll see the groin, and then
The bigger water.' Gently I adjusted
My friend, like a compass needle, towards the shore.
He clutched his stick. I took his arm,
This old man six years younger than my father,
And like my father wounded, like him blind.

Who was he? Now he's dead he comes
Sharply into focus, yet I cannot
Interpret him, not simple saint or fool.
What I knew was an old man in Islington
Who gave me everything he had in mind;
Who loved his language first, the tongue
Of Donne and Swift, and loved it last as well,
However many detours he took home
Along the English road, out of a fastness
That never understood him. His England
Had its own radicals, with their honed passions
Speaking plainly to plain-hearing men.
They were what he was made of, he became
One of their brotherhood, and shares their hearth.

VIII

Even a brief visit cannot exclude her,
My dark mother, who confused my blood.
How old she is now! Like the shawled Indians
Who used to mumble rosaries when she sneaked me
To church without my parents' knowing.
She said the Latin spells over and over.
What did they mean? I knelt at her elbow,
My eyes took in a hunched scrum of old women,
With soles calloused and chapped like baked soil.

The editor handed back my review:
Why write peasant Spanish,
A man like you, with your education?
Send it to me in English. I'll get it translated
By someone who sins less against the language.

If I could introduce him to my teacher!
I have only her to blame,
Her and her village – Cuacalco, under the squat hill.
One time she took me to see where she grew up –
Without a father, I later deduced; where she bore
Her one child without a husband, left him
To an aunt when my father gave her work.
And how she worked! Dark mother, dark grandmother,
Fed me, kept me clean, let me ride on her back,
Taught me her language, told me her story
Time after time, always the same words,
Yet the same words real as though she'd just found them.
I was the stand-in for her dismal baby,
She called me *hijo*; last time I visited
She took for granted I was her only son.

She's not poor now. At market
They call her Doña, step aside to let her pass
But behind her back say *hechicera*, witch,
Her herbs and charms are famous. She gets
Chickens, coins, tin amulets for her intercessions,
She cures the neighbourhood. Her saints

Hear her without fail. She has her faith
As other folk have air to breathe, yet asks
Nothing for herself. She cannot read or count.
She has forgotten nothing in eighty years.

I know the powdery fields she worked as a girl, the *jacales*
Wearing tin or tile roofs slanted to black
Doorless openings, the irregular pulse
Of animal and human habitation, smoke rising
Straight on breezeless days like stems of gold,
At mountain-height dilating in blue.
The church, begun in 1612, never completed, barks
Its two bells, the women kneel,
Drunk with labour, prayer and the scent
Of arum lilies, incense, stale wax, flesh.
Their children hang on them like fruit.
Bead-eyed madonnas and their Christs survey
The ragged flock franchised by the beatitudes.

There was, she said, a snake – and claimed she'd seen it –
They call it pasture-snake there in her *tierra*.
It lives on milk. When it finds cows grazing
It writhes up a leg and fastens to an udder,
Drawing until the cow is dry.
When a nursing mother falls asleep,
The snake comes, fastens to the breast,
Giving the child its tail for pacifier.
If it comes just once, the child won't live.

Even the briefest visit home cannot exclude her,
Though now she always cries when I see her and needs
More love than I have, so I give her money.
Some debts, when language fails, have to be settled crudely –
When love and language fail.

IX

The long blind wall towards Oxford pebble-dashed,
Moss-blotched, veined with ivy; a gravel drive
Unraked, visited by nurses and by me
Who leaned my bicycle against a trellis,
Rang at the blank door.
                              You left the chain on,
Sprung the latch, with a 'Yes?' like a hinge being forced,
Always in dark glasses, glamorous, faded.
'When I first met you,' I said on my third visit,
'I thought you were your daughter.'
'We chose not to have children,' you said,
'And kept our youth for a time. Now we're old.'
He slept on a bed in the living room (could hardly move –
You'd abandoned the top storey years before).
Blind to the north, to the south the house
Took in with its wide windows all of Berkshire.
He lay stone-deaf, like the battered river-god you'd find
At an ancient spring, gazing on treetops, cloudscapes,
At night the embers of the living towns.

From such a height it hardly looked like England,
Scored by the calligraphy of ancient roads
And tiled with variegated fields that seemed the bed
Of a broad pool peculiar to one palace. 'Just before
We came home from Persia, father had it built.
It's cleverly done.'
                          Heat swam
Like water over the Berkshire plain.
You were already blind except to misprints, certain flowers.
Concise, precise, civil, unsentimental, abstract words
Throng to describe you, like so many doves
Loosed from neglect to a hand that scatters bread.
They seek you not because you were over eighty
And abstractions love old age and the dead,
But since you brought to bear on your tradition
Purities of logic, Persian, mathematics,
Tools that served you, as you thought, supremely.
I typed and re-typed your last essay, 'The Roots

Of Unity', from large-scale handwriting on lined sheets
Like a child's crude exercise –
Phrases and formulae like the root system
Of a plant grown wise and beautiful, and frail
So it sends thin fingers out to hold.
                                        Perhaps they hold,
I cannot understand them, though I know for you
Logic was a passion, commanding fever as the flesh will do,
Or as those windows took command of Berkshire.

'We had a proper garden.' How unlike English pastoral
Your acres must have been, though starred and stained
With familiar blooms. Even now the banks and rusty lawns
Make sense in terms of everything around them,
Interpreting, not distorting, their context.
If, when I entered your cool, dazzling rooms
I seemed to step out of the present tense,
It was only history I wiped off my shoes on the mat
To enter stable time: season, solstice, fruit,
As Horace did, leaving Rome for his Sabine farm,
Cooling his wrists in a spring unfenced, unfouled.
'We get up with the sun. Most of the winter we sleep.'
Aloof from the *blind nurses of racial character*
You evolved a mystic disregard for commerce,
For war, assassination; instead adhered
To what does not change, is not destroyed,
What you share with Sumer, Greece and Alexandria,
With Amherst, Weimar. Hampton Court,
Curious territory no single map contains,
A *Geist* without race, which cannot be annexed,
Enjoined, perverted, a refinement
Hungry for forms and the few sharp timeless truths.

The *barren severities* of history, Persia taught you,
Made no lasting wound on a real culture,
Any more than the adjustments of an intellectual border
Affected the capital of human sense –
As if Darwin, Marx and Freud had not clouded the sky
With their unsettling breath; how long have they lived
Compared with Homer? What is their style,
Have they really touched language or only words?

Would this plane, this beech,
This cypress tree survive in Eden or Utopia,
Or only here?
                    The mind is a garden, as the garden is,
And hangs above a wilderness it comprehends.
To lose sight, to see the garden fade out gradually,
Not because it changes, but we change,
Brings round the last term of old wisdom, death,
Clean of fear and superstition.
The tiny islands of pleasure, the reefs where love ran aground
Are lost, each private temple falls, and yet,
As you knew they would, the week you died
The flowers kept their scent,
And not a word you wrote became less true.

X

I don't keep up with your wives, the sisters:
How are they? One dead? Both dead? Your broken daughter,
Does she still wander around her locked and loving hostel
Looking for you, or a tree, or any sharp thing?
That night at your house she stared at me and stared
And you said how when she was three the eczema
Had eaten off her innocence; you clutched her
Night after night like a starfish to your chest
So she would not chew herself, so she would not bleed.
And you kept her as long as you could, she grew to a girl,
To a young woman with dark, unsettled eyes
Who played with gas- and water-taps; once, naked,
Got out into the street, wandered down the hill
Curious about the way her skin changed colour
When she walked under the trees, and in shade changed texture
As gooseflesh came in the chill and subsided in sunlight.

The night I came to your house, the power cuts –
It was the three-day week – returned the hill to Keats's century.
No cars, no jaundiced street-lamps, only
Candle-light through curtains; gaslight, firelight.
When I knocked you answered the door holding a candle
In one of those brass dishes with an ear and lip.
By candlelight you let me see your pictures –
Bottles, most of them, not like Morandi's
But made of light and oil, of breasts, of skin.
Faint, ghostly – how they haunt me; some critics called them,
When they showed them at the Tate to mark your death –
Called even the late ones, even the ones where red
Bursts in like fire, or rage – 'serene' and 'cold',
As though the distance from the canvas
Imposed by brush, by fingers, and the hours
You spent before them cooled the focused passions
That punished your gentle body, your handsome face
In those fast weeks, as the cancer ate you,
Even that time, two months before your death.

While we talked you kneaded little lumps of wax
Between your restless finger-tips, then lost them.
'And my poems,' you said, patting a pile of them.
'I've spent the last twelve months getting them into order.
They're numbered, and the sequence matters –
At least,' you added, like a boy, glanced shyly
Out of the dark window at the dark, 'at least
I believe it matters, there is an argument.'
The poems – 'They will not sell.' They have not sold.

Where did they come from? Who chose the bottles?
What caused the uncompromised heart of this dead man?
First the huge silence, then love and its implements –
Palette, knife, tubes, blank canvas like stillest water
Of a lagoon waiting a shaping breath;
And on the table, cool surfaces of glass.
How could you exclude
Memory, or love, or the broken child?
Your paintings move from grace and natural hunger
To pain, and death too has its palette.
Those sleepless nights you fought with your fallen angel
And lost have marked you. You remain awake
For ever, like a figure out of Dante.

It's winter; the lights will not come on
In that stark memory. I walk down the hill.
He is dying. I carry in my satchel
His poems, his and Piper's Venice,
And in a red card binding
'The Impact of Architecture': *If we speak*
On occasion of an eye-window, it is not
To suggest that it sees but that a break
In the wall is like a socket. Buildings
Are images of blindness . . . At midnight
The lights came on, I had walked half way home.
I read his essay on the tube and he was dying
Even as I puzzled at it. His city was dying,
The hill was burning, glowing like a coal,
Flaring and cooling towards the morning, and I
Was twenty-four. Urbino I had not seen. Rapallo

I have not seen. I've read now – watching his mouth,
Watching his dancing hands – his Rimini, his Florence.

We are waiting for Ruskin, for Pater, your natural family.
When they home from their travels you'll emerge
At your white door with its Georgian fanlight,
But then in broad daylight. 'Where have you been?' you'll say.
Waiting for the right time, which is now, you're at last
Released from the hostel of neglect; your mother is gone
And your daughter, your wives, the world of women.
Here are your canvases, the bottles replenished
With claret and white light, with amber, green.
The world that made you has at last gone down;
You are released to this unmaking world
By your pliant lucidity and those
Discreet charged images that flare.
'They will not sell.' Not yet, they will not sell.

XI

Is there a limit to how many changes
A man can go through between his first love
And the one that bursts his heart?
And with those changes, a kaleidoscope of views –
From cellars and high balconies, sober and drunk –
Always the same city flanked by the same hills,
Washed by a sea as filthy as the shore.
But the rough boys grew suave; cheap fashions bought them,
Poor mutants of affluence and bigotry.

Each year, it seems to me, you altered colour –
Not as the chameleon to hide
But to be vivid like an ulcer or a bloom.
I follow after and – two decades late –
Look for your footprints in the shantytowns.
Here are the children of the child you loved
In endless transformations as he was,
And I see what dragged you in and out of guilt
Like a fish on a sharp hook but a weak line:
You boarded the midnight tram to what you wanted
Regardless of the price – which was your life.

I met you once at a reception in London
Held in a low-ceilinged room by the river
With writers you despised. You approached me
And said, 'How very English of you: an umbrella,
On such a night as this!' In your smile
I counted the teeth. I'd come down from Oxford
Not to hear you but Auden.
I'd not even seen your films, much less read
A word of yours in verse or prose.
You had a haggard look, also a hunger
To be out of there, back in your element.
I didn't understand your manner. 'Goodnight.'
I hurried off to Paddington for the train.

I wish I'd lingered at least a few minutes
In your solitude that evening in London,

Simply to learn your voice, to taste
The ashes of Casarsa from your lips. What errors,
What pain it might have helped me round, to hear
Just for a moment in that crowded room
The pure elixir of your egotism,
The Italy that coarsened your tongue with love.

XII

Greek, Latin and Italian were required
For Comp. Lit. 201. I had Latin
And elementary perjury. They got me
(Like some others) into the dark
Upholstered room.
                     He sat, drowsy, possessed,
Not at the table head but at the long side,
Like Christ among disciples, mainly girls.
In our different hearts we worshipped him;
He smelled as sweet to us
As Alexander on the field of battle,
His heavy-lidded eyes steady as a falcon's.

We addressed – or he did – Narrative,
The epic observed by lyric eyes
('The only eyes we have these days').
The course that should have sped from Homer down
Through Virgil to Dante, Milton, Perse
(Whose *Birds* he rendered, with Braque's lithographs)
Stalled somewhere in *Odyssey* Book IV.

'Forget the *genre*, epic's not Homer's word –
And anyway, who was he?' We read Lord
And Parry, learned to doubt, while he recited.
'Forget the page, hear the words in air.'
He hung them there like notes
From staves of silence our attention made.
'We ought to shut all but the book of memory,
But leave that open like an ear.'
                     The Muse was real
To Homer and to him, Penelope not a trope
But a weaver whose desire
Plucked notes from the loom, and a lover back
From deep water, deep time, even out of death's
Cavern, where Virgil followed, and then Dante.
There he now squats on the hollow hill
Instructing them.
                In the course of other adventures,

In another country, I am reminded of you
By your death. Haven't I thought of you before
In twenty years?
                        Once, maybe,
On the spoiled site of Ilium
Where I could have gathered sacks of clam-shells.
I reflected on the diet of Homer's tedious characters
And sensed how far I was from your Homer's world.
Your death now simply tells me I've forgotten
The word is sacred. I've grown out of it
Into the secular.
                        Once you assessed
Some poems. I gave you forty. 'I read the first
And thought there's really something here.
It wasn't there in the other thirty-nine.'
Did I thank you? Now I thank you: elegy,
Imagined reparation.
                        In memory you're not dead
But away on your blue island, practising
A hundred voices against the inattentive tide.
In the *Odyssey* Zeus speaks early on, 'The poem's
Airborne almost at once'; for many, you were the first
To make the sequence of words we call a poem
Audible; you moved us more than an instrument,
Zeus of our adolescence, maker, mover,
Yet I remember not one line of yours.

It is winter, my idols have all shed their leaves.
There is no fruit, no shade, a weight of snow
And, caused by death to think of you, a weight
Of sadness that falls short of grief.

Here are some faded notes from my spiral book,
The page headed 'Homer, Virgil, Dante'
And underneath, 'hero, patriot, priest'.
'Battle was made for poets; if they were true,
Words blinded them until they saw with words,
Leaving the sharpened vision of poems.'
'Poets, like Iopas, may live to have white hair,
Harps of gold, and kings to listen
While taking loving census of their slaves.'

I'm sure you never said such stuff, it was me
Sententiously mishearing, I always did. I do.
Yet without malice, played on by your voice.
Auden says the poem reads us. You might have said
The poem makes us worth reading.
Love is somewhere near the poet, jealous,
Seated beside him, beside you, across the table, in dark
Recesses, folded tight on its deception,
Hungry in devotion, watching, writing,
Its corpse quite bare beneath its ignorant toga.

XIII

I opened my porthole the first morning
Intending to say *ma'haba* to the Nile
And a yellow mouse jumped into my sleeping sheet.
I checked out of the youth hostel barge
And into a hotel on 26 July Street.

Waiting for you I had two days to kill.
My map was all in French. After an hour at the wrong
Bus stop, I was appropriated by Farid Fahmy,
A teacher keen to try his English. He talked me up
The Citadel, the Sultan's sequinned mosque,
Ibn Tulun, El Mu'ayyad, El Azhar,
The medersa, the suqs; at last we came
To rue El Hassan and climbed to his flat
High on a cliff of habitations,
A crumbling summit where we sat in shadow.
There were no doors on his storey. It was held in common.
We ate orange quarters cooled in water,
Served in a blue bowl by a palsied aunt.
On the balcony his kid brother took my elbow
And pointed out the sights. I met his doves.
The boy lifted one out of its rustic cote
Gently, as if handling a flower,
Then hurled it at the sky.
Other doves followed in an arc of white
Pure against khaki sand, grey concrete, yellow sky,
Blown upwards, solid flakes of brilliance offered
To the god of hospitality.
                    You and I
Met as planned at Giza, under the trite Sphinx's gaze,
By her right paw. At the Sphinx cafe in town
(It was soon after the Six Day War, the buildings
Were sand-bagged, Israeli jets flew low
Breaking the sound barrier twice a day)
We wondered how we might join *El Fatah*.
I confess I committed murder in my heart
And so did you, we were so hot with virtue,
Remote from the actual sources of our rage.

You get used to talk, to traffic, heat,
The amazing daily ritual of the wealthy
At Groppi's, shovelling ice cream into their boredom.

Each time we stopped on our way up the Nile
We got arrested. As luck would have it,
Your perfect Arabic was suspect. One night
The officers came back for us in a black Mercedes,
Drove us at top speed into the dark,
Braked hard above a scroll of fluid moonlight,
Switched off the ignition and we heard
The unearthly belching chorus of Nile frogs.
The sergeant explained: sometimes his men got bored –
They thought we'd like to hear the serenade.

At Tel-el-Amarna we both fell in love
With a willowy serving-girl whose eyes
Kept meeting ours. You spoke a line of poetry to her
And found she was some sort of boy . . . In the train
(Third-class, half-fare for students)
We were offered hard-boiled pigeon-eggs
And sung to, touched, our foreignness and pallor
A talisman. We slept as they did
On luggage racks . . . One place
We crossed the river in a brown felucca
Like a dragonfly blown slowly over sunlight
And found the tombs we'd come for
Defaced with bright official slogans about the future.
Returning, we were pursued by a gang of kids who chanted
Israeli, Israeli, and levelled stones at our heads.
I have a scar, the only wound from my engagements there.

By donkey into the Valley of Kings, past the stumps
Of Ozymandias' legs; in Karnak
High on a wall of the holy of holies the word
Rimbaud cut deep in stone; by the Pool of Frogs
And a huge pink granite scarab among papyruses
We took mint tea and a shisha, served by another androgyne . . .
The moon came up red, floating out of the palms
Huge as Achilles' shield, in the sky, in the pool,
Praised by ecstatic frogs, climbed clear of the tallest

40

Column, the last lotus capital, and began to cool.
We watched it go to coin size, turn white,
Silver white; we sipped mint tea,
Scalding our hearts, then scalding them again.

XIV

You taught me chess when I was six,
Just so you'd have someone to beat
In a leisurely way, not so I'd take much notice.
You advanced white pawns and knights until at evening
My queen fell to your bishop, my king resigned.
Formally you shook hands, muttered a German phrase.
We climbed to supper. A servant cleared the board.

When you were twelve and broke your leg
Your father beat you first for carelessness
Then summoned the physician. Prussia
Claimed your little homeland five years later.
The Emperor came right past your front door
Requiring homage, riding rather badly
On a huge horse proportioned for a statue.

You fled the Imperial Recruiting Officer,
The wars he had in mind not wars you'd choose.
Once on the road, you fled for decades.
My favourite failure! Like me a youngest son,
Deserter, optimist; dear, reluctant modern man, uprooted
From the tall family house by Pauleskirche
With office and stores at street level, and above,
The family rooms, almost prosperous,
Silent with formal tensions, sleeves and collars
Getting frayed but rigid with starch
And grey as dough. Uprooted
From the narrow garden
That plunged to the brisk, unfriendly river . . .

You fled west with the human flood of disaffection,
Settled in Kansas, then Colorado, down the map
To Mexico, then south, then further south . . .
Dogged still by history – Prussia, Pancho Villa,
Liquidators, conscience: almost prosperous
Time after time, shopkeeper, impresario, clerk;
Almost destitute.
                    Failure's hero, you could not acknowledge

The huge vindictive goddess riding her storm cloud
Behind your little billowing wake of dust
Down the spine of both Americas
Until your final venture failed in Chile.

Five decades of declining years
Under the kind, unjudging care of my aunts,
And the President of the United States himself,
The Irish one, *und auch Papistisch*,
Wished you a happy century.
And even that was not the end of it
At Mar Vista, your dogs, hours on the porch just swinging
On the plaid garden seat. I was presented to
Old ladies you were allowed to court.
There was your case of rusty books, the regimented
Gothic tombstones of your complete, uncut Goethe,
And you subsiding into German.

You so enjoyed chess with me! I've forgotten the rules
But keep the tone in mind of your guttural
Crowing when you won. It pleased me to surrender
My little Saxon king with his pellet of lead ballast
That kept him upright in the evening breeze. I've fled as far
East as you fled west. Conscription, history, accident
And the vindictive goddess riding home
Mistaked me for you.
                              You'd recognize this house
If you came to the door tonight. You'd like to stay.
I have your chessmen in a box on the piano.
You'd know just where I've been, where I am bound to,
But being as you are, you'd spread the board.
We'd play in silence and you'd not let on.

XV

It wasn't snowing but it should have been.
You were an old man, nine months from the grave.
Your hand was very dry and very hot
And large, as I recall (I was a boy,
Fourteen years at most, I led you round
Part of the school, your guide; you seemed to listen).
That night you read in a slow, dismissive voice
That left the words like notes on staves hung in the air,
No longer yours, but part of memory –
You talked about Miss Dickinson of Amherst
And said aloud the eight lines of her poem
'The heart asks pleasure first'. And from that night
I've known the poem word-perfect, part of me.

I think you let more lines free into language
And memory with your rusty, lonely voice
Than any other poet of our age.
It must have been like freeing doves
And watching them go off to neighbouring cotes
Or into the low clouds of your New Hampshire
Knowing they'll meet no harm, that they'll survive
Long after the hand that freed them has decayed.

Those lines are wise in rhythm and they lead
Into a clapboard dwelling, or a field,
Or lives that prey upon the land and one another,
Or the big country where we both were children.

XVI

Idols, icons, dust; those hideous
Counter-Reformation Jesuses
Whose brows are purple thorn-cushions, hands pierced
As if candle-wax had oozed
Thickening from the wounds, the feet, the side;
Fingers too fine to be a carpenter's . . .

Yours weren't: your impatient little hands indifferently
Healed wood or clay, as a doctor's might.
You taught yourself. 'I had to start somewhere,
So I did forgeries. Quite good ones, too.'
You styled yourself 'artist'. A restorer
Is artist, I suppose, in the sense a skilled
Editor once in his life's a poet, when he reads
Through ten corruptions a first clarity.

I left your stale apartment always sneezing
As if I'd been in a mine. I blew my nose
And made clay-coloured stains on the white linen.

Your two rooms held two families: in the first
Seven children coted in bunk beds
And your own double bed like an unkempt mainland,
Heart of that stifling archipelago;
Your wife with young amusing eyes and a body
That hung on her heavily, like dough,
And kept surprising you with births, miscarriages
And illness – she brought us tea
In gilded cups from her black scullery . . .
And then the second room: the coffin-sized radio-victrola
With its sea-green hearth-light, an L of seats,
Your books in heaps on which the dust
Established colonies and spread on spider highways
Up to the ceiling with its dim fruit of light;
And the shelves, the boxes where the saints and Christs
– Most of them in transit – gloomily
Waited your touch, when their wings or haloes
Were readjusted, or the cross affixed

To shoulder or heart again, the eyes
Renewed with beads like tiny marbles,
To be sold, or sent back to their churches . . .
They didn't interest me. I came to you
For idols, talk of idols, talk of ruins;
You knew them all, each Pre-Columbian site,
And though you liked them less than the saints and angels,
They were your livelihood as trafficker, restorer.
They had no temples to return to now.
History betrayed them into objets d'art.

I like to think my weekly visits
Renewed your pagan interests: when you played
A few notes on a Mixtec ocarina
Your poor, unsanctified rooms became a temple.
At your suggestion we finally travelled
South and east, to see, never to buy.

You cradled those terracotta corpses,
Some brightly painted and some
Grey-brown like your own tired skin,
Gingerly, with superstition, with resentment, too,
That they remained strange and would not come clear.
You were willing to sell them to a young collector
But felt, as well, for all your generous knowledge –
More than a scholar's, knowledge of the palm
And finger-tip, the nose, the tongue –
Each sale an infidelity to them:
Not that you did not know their value;
You did not know their meaning, and that hurt you.
'What god is this? From the beaked mouth
It might suggest Ehecatl, the wind;
And yet the stylized foot belongs to the war-god.
Why then does he carry maize and a rattle,
What are those holes in his brow?'
'Are you sure you married up the proper fragments
Or is this a new god, drawn from several idols?'
I took it home, catalogued it 'Veracruz' –
The province you came from, and your sons all have
Totonac features; I had statuettes
From the thirteenth century they might have modelled for.

Your history has been plundered of its facts
Yet its blood flows, without memory, sometimes pure.

It must be strange to start from ignorance
And gather fragments of a shattered world,
Paste them together, add missing ears and arms,
Then sell them, strangers you have come to know
Intimately, but without a name.

You took me once to Merida. We spent
Days at the Mayan ruins and in churches.
One afternoon we visited a brothel (at thirteen
I did not know a brothel from a café).
You liked a big girl and went with her.
When you'd been gone ten minutes I got worried,
Followed down the dull-lit corridor
To where, at the end, over a half-door like a bar-door,
I saw you mounted on her like a locust
Perched feeding on a bloated aubergine.
I was suspended between nausea and laughter
To see you there so earnestly at work
Fitting yourself to that tumescent body,
Restorer! you were in your middle fifties
Under the little neon cabinet
In which an icon stared out like a fish
Into the distance of its own reflection.
That evening we went to Kabah: palaces
Of Tlaloc with the rain-god's stylized beaks
Hung like quotation-marks in stone, suggesting
'Temple', 'Hallway', 'Sacrifice'. 'You need
A guide?' 'Not us, no thanks,' you said, and yet
The Mayan boy took me by the elbow
And guided me to what he called the 'catacomb'.
Then rain, out of the blue, it seemed, unseasonal,
Confined us in a corbelled passageway
Startled by lightning, and the boy's face close,
His hand firm on my arm, him whispering
Words in his language, I supposed, while you called to me,
Thinking you'd lost me, and I couldn't answer –
*Speluncam Dido dux et Troianus eandem
Deveniunt*, as if Virgil had dumped me there.

The rain stopped, the boy released me.
My pulse was altered, we walked arm in arm –
His profile was off the friezes at Palenque,
His language had survived an ended culture –
Until we found you sketching in evening light.
We walked towards the highway and the dark
Began to smoke down on us; then the fireflies,
Erratic as my pulse, turned ground to heaven
With their rushing green-and-silver starlight.
Nobody had anything to say.
We hitched a ride back, left the boy half way.

I saw your workshop sign on Insurgentes
Last time I was home, and through your window
Your son Jose at work with tools. On what?
I should have called.
Odd how much of one is inadvertently
Borrowed, not acknowledged or returned.
I should have asked for news of both of us,
Rung at your dark apartment for strong tea
In a gilded cup, the gramophone; and, yes,
On the steep common balcony, your wife's
Green parakeets in their shrill tenements.

XVII

Being twelve was something, after all:
'Four o'clock,' he wrote, 'the twenty-fifth.
Calle del Buen Tono 347.
Punctually.' The writing feathered, frayed,
The hand of an old man, brisk but trembling.
'I cannot teach you Nahuatl, but if
You're half as dedicated as you suggest
I can advise. Bear this in mind, however:
No language is given apart from the one
The infant sucks in with a mother's milk.'
As though that mattered! He had written back!
I felt as if the good Lord had consented
To a brief audience with his altar-boy.

I lifted his books down in armfuls from my shelves.
I'd been collecting them for two years – thirty volumes.
Which would I ask him to inscribe? I cut the pages
And bent the spines of each so he'd know I'd read them.

It was the fourteenth when his note came.
I had eleven days, hardly time to change
Into the boy who'd posted that 'dedicated' letter.
I started turning page after page of his scholarship,
Soon yawned, stared at all I had to do and did not do it,
Imagining instead how he would be,
As if his disciplines would have spared an actual man!
Could I become his apprentice and absorb
What he knew of Aztec, Otomi,
Of the little languages, and Greek and Latin,
Hebrew, Persian, Sanskrit? ('We cannot
Value our own or know how tall we stand
Without knowing the world.') One critic wrote,
'He was old even before Babel and for fun
Devised the tongues that divide men,
Exchanging them with God for the gift of years.'

My father's chauffeur drove me down through suburbs
So drab I shut my eyes. As we drew near

The Calle del Buen Tono, children pointed,
Indicating which way we should go.
The only unfamiliar traffic in these streets
Came hunting out their old priest, Father Angel.

I arrived 'punctually'. He was still out –
On his rounds among the hungry and illiterate, I supposed.
Yet his books were there, crowding every wall.
Two very small old women, swaddled in shawls,
Distrustful, fretful, supervised my waiting
Where I sat on a low hard chair, beginning
To see how much he'd written that I'd missed,
How much I'd missed in any case.
Through three rooms (the doors wouldn't close for books)
A solid library of his tongues.

He translated Greek badly, Latin badly;
The Aztec he rendered as though
The nineteenth century had dawned yesterday
In all its brutal freshness on the heart.
But he knew the Aztec language perfectly from books
Having transcribed the chronicles, annotated
The sacred hymns, the prayers, the chants of war;
He was Sahagún and every lesser witness,
Ghosting the figures buried in the silt
Of histories that History had displaced.

I'd not imagined rooms
So dusty, cold, so inhospitable,
Rooms like a dictionary, without waste
Or scruple, good manners or good cheer.
Then he appeared before me and I rose
Too quickly for politeness, more like fear.
His arms hugged his chest, as if he was cold in a shroud,
His hands and face were bleached, his beard, his eyes too seemed
All whites. I never saw a creature so bloodless,
As though he had strayed out of the past,
Or a cloud, or a grave. 'Don Angel!' I exclaimed,
Unfolded his reluctant hand
And did what the Indians do, I kissed it.
And then I blushed because I wasn't Roman Catholic

Or Christian. For the first time in my life
I smelled on him the stale scent
Of utter solitude and abstinence,
Of a man without vanity of the flesh,
Of Jerome, the smell of the desert,
The lonely scholar and the chaste shepherd.
What were his angels? Angels without wings,
The lame and halt, the kind whose place in heaven
Is guaranteed by the beatitudes.

One of the women brought sour coffee on a tray.
We had little to say. He found me out
With two or three sharp questions.
He was not angry that he'd wasted time
On such a green hypocrisy; there was
Only illusion, not malice, in my visit.
I had no discipline, no faith, and that was clear,
Nothing but a boy's ephemeral charm; to him
There was no music but philology, not sun
But candle-light.
                    I stood in the poor street
Outside the scholar's house. Father Angel
Did not see me off; I'd said goodbye
And he turned on a swivel chair back to his work,
Transcribing manuscripts so old,
Each time he turned a page they dwindled further
Towards that extinction which he chronicled.

I felt how distant my home was from his,
And being twelve was not so very much.
I left behind that day, in a heartless house,
One future I was sure I wanted.
Still on my shelves I have his books, and now
I've read them, and he's dead; yet he does appear
Out of the English snow, out of stale study air
From time to time, not to haunt, but qualify
My seriousness, to say, 'You are not a boy any longer.'
He is pale and bloodless with the purity of exile –
The exile of the dead from pure vocation.

XVIII

The huge melons were split and each of us –
Man and boy – got a whole chilled half with rings
Of black and brown pips set in orange flesh,
Succulent after the desert day.

Were the fruit in fact so large
Or is it that I was small
And he, turning his hemisphere
Between the hands that magicked cape and sword,
Said, 'It's like the Toreo.' 'Look at those dark hats!'
With his knife he scraped them from the heart,
Then gingerly dug out the first, best sweetness.

On the long verandah, after arguments and tall tales,
Away from the sunlight's slow combustion, in the stale
Smoke of cooking fires and men's sweat, evening
Began to imitate the bougainvillea –
The sky bruised, darkened.
It was time then to shower before dinner
And everyone went together, since the last
Were likely to be left soaped when the tank had drained.
I was first and lingered by the skirt of spray
To watch my idols come out of the shadows
And cover their naked skin with a suit of lights.
My world had been of women; here were men,
One man especially, the best matador
I ever saw, an Indian, a god, grown rich,
With an unexpected voice, shrill as a cat's,
A cat's courage and its several lives.

That day with *capote* and *muleta*
It had pleased him to dazzle us. It was a *tienta*
Where they test livestock to see how strong the blood is.
Matadors practise without the need
To kill or count applause, as a virtuoso might
Bow to silence, adjust the stool
And play his best preludes to an empty room.
He dazzled us all the same, we were hoarse with cheering,

Until an enormous creature with splayed horns
Pinned him against a *burladero*,
Kept butting, butting him for a full minute.
We carried him gently, as though an angel had fallen.
'I'm not hurt,' he said. That he had to say it
Meant he was hurting, but it was his business.
We lay him on a bench in the shade and fanned him.
Then he walked off by himself beyond the stables.

'How are you now?' I asked when he came to bathe.
He showed me on the skin the horns' abrasions,
Two long burns like grill-marks scorched on steak.
'A little to either side and the kidneys might have been
Unhappy tonight,' he said, then he showed me over
Each of the twenty scars on calf, thigh, groin.
It was a map, each gore a history. 'And the worst
Was this one,' a little livid ridge, he winced to see it.
I stared, repelled and choked by love, considering
A body wounded and risen from its ashes
Twenty times, to triumphs I had witnessed.
Later I managed to ask, 'Could I be a matador?'
He'd seen my first clumsy cape-work that morning.
'How can I tell? I'd have to study your form.'
Then, because he was an Indian and liked me,
'I doubt it. It isn't in your blood.'

Next day we rode out to the steep grazing,
Chose bulls for the *corrida* at Tijuana.
After that they rounded up three cross-bred calves
And herded them into the ring. 'What for?' 'You'll see.'
They roped and felled them, one at a time, and held
The hind legs wide, slit the scrotums with a razor,
And pressed out pearly, tear-shaped testicles.
The empty bags they tied with string, the bullocks
Struggled to their feet and trotted out.
Hardly a drop of blood on the cowmen's hands.
That night around the fire they cooked and ate,
The firelight's pulse playing on their faces.

A week of those heads crescented with death,
Dancing at you, then away, enraged, their autism

Deceived and punished into art – a week among
Interpreters of peril and cruel grace,
Evenings on the long verandah, under large framed photos
Of famous bulls and fighters, staled adventure:
Once there were many giants, now only one,
Companioned with shadows, ghosts at grass, ghosts
Feebly working beside him with cape and sword.
I had arrived too late at the arena:
My hero was now cheaply garlanded.
Had he died, I would have died, I was sure of that.
Such was the love I had those nights I sat
Beside him, or close at his feet, those days
Riding behind him and his twenty scars.
Now, when I think of him, I don't see his face,
But the livid scar, his worst, that looked like the lid
Of a dead eye. I am repelled
And no less choked by love.

XIX

It was late summer, Friday, four o'clock,
The light-stunned Alameda. He ambled through,
Nodding to the vendors, the corporal,
The sweeper, photographer, the gaudy women.
Of the Spanish exiles I remember only him –
A poet with a king's surname, though he was Republican.
His Christian name was Lion.
King and lion, but a common man:
In my clothing sleeps the dust of every highway
And the sweat of many agonies.
Suddenly he comes upon us, spreads his arms
As if to fly, embraces us, then takes
My father by both hands: 'Don Carlos!'
'You've not met my youngest, Leon? My second family.'
'I should be so lucky as to have only two!'
He takes my hand more willingly than it's given
And I avert my face, he rests his hand
First on my head and then my shoulder. How
Lightly it weighs, and how lightly he was passing
Along the promenade, looking left and right
For Spain, and his youth, his heart, his fantasy
Of unbribed justice; how very lightly
He flies, as a stone flung from a crater
After the first turbulence flies cooling
Until it could be a bird, and then it falls.

When I visited Segovia years later
I saw a castle like a great ship poised
To sail on air, but made of stone
The way so many dreams translate in stone,
In prose, in blood, in history, and go down.

The weight of his hand, and in rustling sunlight
Their voices – now both dead – talking as friends,
And I never knew
My father had such friends (as when he quoted
Victor Hugo in French, only once in our life

Speaking French, quoting verse, leaving me at a loss
With a stranger I thought I knew, of whom I'm made).

As poet and man he played cleanly,
Without trick or miracle, his seemingly marginal role,
Singing *the Destined Song which the stars won't forget*
And his people will stumble upon, and unearth themselves
In him, as I do when I recollect
That promenade with my father, that hand on my head
Resting as the priest's does on my son's head at the rail;
But we were in bright daylight by the bandstand,
He smoked a cheroot, he did not bless
But attached me by a blighted succession
To a tideless war, to his Troy abandoned by dazed
Warriors with no luggage but their language
And found in exile echo, and its echo.

XX

Lantana clouded a hill in each of your worlds,
Weaving the slope with gritty fibres, giving a blur of hue.
Here in your final world the cluster stars of pink and yellow
Outstay you in their dark of sticky leaves.
The scents cling still of your hair and hands in the room
That speculates on pines and palms, the crazy woodpeckers
Drilling their acorns in and out, a shattering jay.
That speculates alone without your eyes.

Never having shared this house with you
It has become less alien now you've left it.
Like me bereaved, it will revive in time.
The trees will alter, and the shade until
Nothing's quite the same, yet it will retain you
Even when the furniture arranges itself
Around other lives. At least this one wide bedroom
Is yours for good, with its gaze on the steep trees,
The violent mimosa flared at the fence and further
A huge Pacific with two tankers moving
So slowly they'll never get to port.

Calhoun, Capistrano, Coyoacan – together
We left behind so many worlds before I left you,
But never in this way and never again. The brass
Casket of ashes (warm from the sun) we laid
In a box with flowers from your garden, lowered it
On ropes into a hole of statutory depth.
Two bored Chicanos tamped the earth hard, laid the turf
Back over, leaving hardly a scar. Good surgeons!
She is alive. I read the psalm. I feel her pulse.

After twenty years of 'flying visits',
My 'pressing affairs' and 'I can spare about a week',
You're hardly stranger dead than when you lived,
But for this sadness like a fog I can't see through
That will not clear, that rises from your body;
Or a smoke of death, and scentless,
The air of love now visible, milk-white.

If I had heart I'd number all the losses.
It's the real love I wasted. Even when I chose
Exile in resentment it was there. I knew it given
And only death could take it, which it has,
Setting it where it echoes like a call
Morning, evening, now. If I try to walk,
As an infant risks first steps towards coaxing arms,
I fall half way, and take amiss the loving laughter.
Rubbing my eyes I rise and try again.